SETTLEMENT POEMS 2

BY
KRISTJANA GUNNARS

WINNIPEG: TURNSTONE PRESS, 1980

SETTLEMENT POEMS 2

Canadian Cataloguing in Publication Data

Gunnars, Kristjana, 1948–
  Settlement poems 2

  ISBN 0-88801-051-6

  1. Icelanders in Manitoba – Poetry.
I. Title.
PS8563.U55S482   C811'.54   C81-091023-3
PR9199.3.G85S482

Contents

Settlement Poems began after a visit with Prof. Sveinn Skorri Höskuldsson of the Department of Nordic Studies at the University of Iceland. His encouragement led to the research behind these poems. Historical sources were found in the National Library of Iceland in Reykjavik, where Olafur Hjartar kindly copied sections of the Library's holdings for me. Other historical sources were found at the Special Icelandic Collection of the Elizabeth Dafoe Library at the University of Manitoba, where Sigrid Johnson was kind enough to copy material for me as well. Acknowledgements are also due to Prof. Eli Mandel of the University of Toronto, who was writer-in-residence for Regina in 1978-79. His enthusiasm and kindness were helpful during the writing of the poems. Final thanks go to David Arnason of St. John's College at the University of Manitoba, whose encouraging response to Volume One was helpful in completing Volume Two.

— Kristjana Gunnars

JÓHANN BRIEM 2, I

20 from the south
are leaving, 1876
the third & last group

gudmundur magnússon from south-
vardgjá is taking his coffin
the one he's had for 14

years, wants the priest
to carry his corpse to church
& put it in the coffin with 3

candles burning on the lid
as soon as he's dead
ólafur briem, carpenter

from grund made
the coffin, shaped like a house
or a lantern, the kind jón

árnason from jökull also
carries with him everywhere
just in case, you know

when a person leaves

life, you have to put him in
the ground somewhere, in

a coffin
a housecoffin, a lantern-
coffin, on this trip ólafur

gudmundsson from arnarbaeli
in ölves interprets

he's been there before

JÓHANN BRIEM 2, II

hannes scheving (dead 1726)
has been unearthed
in the munkathverár-cemetery
inadvertently

jón farmer, curious
has them dig it all up
the coffin strung in black
tanned leather, nailed

tight around the gable-
end with brass tacks
one side of the gable-head
loose where the corpse is

slipped in
for a burial like that
i'd go to new iceland
(when you're poor you're buried

without graveclothes, without
coffin, tied to a thin board)
though it's slow sailing
i can't say

it's bad, this moving over
from old to new iceland
a bit crowded on the boats

& wagons, unusual
food, some stomach
illness, mainly
for the kids, but other-

wise i can't say
it's as bad as the great
smallpox of 1707
& 1786, or the famines

of 1756 & 1784 (with
starvation on every
farm, no one
had anything for any-

one) only
30 or 40 children are dead
of the stomach pain
going to canada (11

in the first group dead
on arrival in winnipeg)
but it's not as bad

as 1785 (when, without
timber, you were buried
without even a board, dumped
with everyone else together

under a cairn
in the black-tanned night
nailed in with brass
stars) not that

bad

JÓHANN BRIEM 2, III

should have tried harder
normally

you're sewn into a linen bed-
sheet (over your head, under
your feet) unless

you're gentry or live
in a village (a priest gets
to go in a cassock

a gentlewoman gets formal
wear, gold-plated belt
others get ordinary

bellies of yearling lambs
sewed on leather shoes)
but everyone gets something

for the last journey, everyone
gets a red, yellow striped
tail-cap & a book to read

(it's a long trip) it's always
been that way
should have tried harder

to fish the poet out of red
river when he fell off
the flatboat, pálmi jónsson

from skagafjördur, might
have been old, infirm
but he was a poet, a homeopathic

doctor, was wise
a wise man
should have jumped in

to retrieve him even if
it's a corpse, a person
needs burial with linen

with cap, with book, should
at least have buried the book
shouldn't have let it

float on its own

JÓHANN BRIEM 2, IV

no aspen armband

(even apparitions
reappear with armrings)

no birch-chip blanket
under, wood-shaving pillow
no one or two psalms

no oak-block pack-saddle
for balance, no funeral
procession, one on each side

of the pony, no one
singing one or two
verses as he passes

by the farm
cap in hand, no arrival
at the churchgate, soulgate

no one of two bells
ringing, no lord's
herbal garden sung

as he passes, sigurdur
hjálmarsson from skagafjördur
carpenter, only thirty

apprenticed carpentry all
his life, gone
into red river with the other

drowned
& what'll he hammer
out of water, the one

we lose a second time

JÓHANN BRIEM 2, V

no, not angelica

she doesn't kill
not the kind that grows
in the mountains in

hjaltastadathinghá

the root jón thorkelsson
from klúka ate
september 6, 1876

wasn't angelica, place

the gravedigging shovels
over him in a cross
carry his coffin around

the church, carry him
on your shoulders, turn him
around three times

clockwise, when the priest
throws open the spades
fill the grave quickly

trample down the mountain
with bare feet, two times

leave his grave flat when you go

let him throw no sundial
shadow when day circles over
when you finish his grave

leave no reminder
of angelica mountains, no
not angelica

she doesn't kill

15

the weather on the day of death
depends on the deceased

a brutal man will be hard
to bury, like bjarni

sýslumadur halldórsson from thingeyri
buried 1773 in hailstorm
(they dropped the coffin head first
into a ditch

where he still lies
on his head, but he was a brutal
man) you go the way
of the life you lead

but anna, why anna the widow
(gudmundsdóttir from stedji
in thelamörk) what has she to do
with the old law

it may not work in new iceland
nothing works

the way anna walks
out on lake winnipeg, late winter
1877, the way she goes

without returning
that's how it is
you disappear out there

& depend nothing on goodness
it will always be brutal
with hail, blizzard

strike hard as if you are

JÓHANN BRIEM 2, VII

don't spare the funeral feast

even if it's sumac
white-flowering, red-
leaved this time of year

august 1877, drink
the staghorn sumac
indian lemonade, clenched

scarlet berries soaked
in water
drink for the dead one

hjörtur jóhannsson from vatnsnes
who practices, swims
lake winnipeg, don't spare

the houseblessing now
burn up the bayberry, bury
his memory in daylight

break new ice, drink
hard (eggert briem says
the drowned one is pleased

when you drink for him)
sumac berry that steeps
swims

for the young boy who cramps
into a tight blood-red fist
who floats in lake winnipeg

flowering now
in thin patches of new ice

JÓHANN BRIEM 2, VIII

a pregnant woman never walks
under the rafters of a new
house (she won't give birth

unless a rafter beam is built
over her bed) she never
walks under a clothesline

(the umbilical cord will tangle
round the baby's neck) she
never combs her hair in bed

(she'll have hard labor)
never sleeps in a ptarmigan-
feather quilt, then

she won't give birth at all
if she won't give birth at all

ptarmigan feathers have to be
stuffed under her hips
still an unmarried man

valdemar sigmundsson from
thingeyjarsýsla builds a new
house, washes his clothes

cuts his hair, catches
game (ptarmigan
the unswimming, cackling bird)

valdemar does everything

(how could he
the most skillful in survival
fall overboard, off
a moving ship on lake

winnipeg, suffocate unsaved
arms, legs, stomach
waterlogged, early september
1877) he'll never

move in
the new house, live
like a pregnant woman

from now on, remember
everything he'll never do

THORLEIFUR JÓAKIMSSON I

take a quick look at espólín's
yearbooks, you'll see life
depends on weather
beasts tumble down dead

& people after, if winter
is severe
have to know what
to expect, have to blow up

a ptarmigan's craw, a cow's
bladder (if it's hard
it'll storm, if soft it'll be
calm, a quick test)

need an old bird's crop
the first winter, 1875
frost, snow from october
22 till april

20, 1876
38 minus, 3 feet
deep in march, try
the old standby

gráskinna: blizzard on new-
year's day, means hard winter
snowfall on paul's mass (january

22) means hard winter
full moon on paul's mass
means hard winter: it works

gráskinna's good as oxbladder
hardly need to look

got it by heart

THORLEIFUR JÓAKIMSSON, DAYBOOK II

august 21, 1876: (heard it
said, survive in the great
plains, survive anywhere)

only just beginning to

learn grasshopper hunting
since april 20, mild

small rain all summer
today is the first large
grasshopper harvest, all

summer at daybreak
picked them off the tops
of tall grass stalks, one

by one, cold, unmoving
in the nightchill, folded wings
mouth-sucking, rubbing

for song: the edge
of a wing across ribs, hind
legs (heard it said

they multiply in big
groups, migrate vast
distances, destroy large

fields, crops) today
prepared a row of dry
grass, a willow broom, swept

the herd sprinkling
into flames in the grass
small rain of insects, charred

in dawn, harvested scorched

today is the first step
on black stubble, warm
after the cold nightspell

i'm only just beginning

THORLEIFUR JÓAKIMSSON, DAYBOOK III

october 7, 1876: more rain
since august, whole days
of rain from the north

september mild, first nightfrost
october, otherwise
easy with cicadas

in the brush, fast moving
wind in the dry rushes
loud rattle of song

of the four-winged cicada
the nonjumping, large, black
seen the eggs in twigs

dead, broken on the ground
seen them feed brown
on roots, crawl treetrunks
easy

to harvest early mornings
pluck away the wings
bring them in, a sack full
for stew, sometimes whole

days i've eaten boiled

cicada from the dry brush
have to stay alive, have to

sing the easy songs, the ones
that flow like rivers, easy

on the memory

THORLEIFUR JÓAKIMSSON, DAYBOOK IV

october 28, 1876: hail, cold
spell from the north
leaves on trees turning

brown, nightfrost now
(jóhann says winter begins
today) end of ant season

learned to roast
grind, winnow ants
into powder, black sugar

big carpenters in dead stumps
simple to pick
by hand, wasp-like

creatures with wings, elbowed
antennae, live like bees
small ones

build mounds with sticks
learned to trap them, place

a box in their settlement
stir up the den
they'll fall in (jóhann says

you can shovel them
into a willow shoot winnowing
tray, cover them with hot
coals, winnow the whole

colony together, says
the coals roast the ants
winnow them, the coals

separate the chaff, the abdomen
falls away)

this insect harvesting won't
last, thorgrímur
would rather starve, or walk

to winnipeg, rather
abandon the colony than
all die together, says

he won't rub elbows

with those who suffer
because it's ugly, but if
you stay, next summer

it won't be ants
it'll be wheat, rye, barley
thorgrímur

just won't wait

THORLEIFUR JÓAKIMSSON, DAYBOOK V

november 29, 1876: icelandic
river froze overnight
november 12, 11 days later

snow 18 inches
deep in the woods
15 minus

been stalking deer, tracks
of separated toes in new
snow, seen them

gallop like rocking horses
wallow like buffalo, some
times seen a white flash

vanish before the wood
heard the far whistle, low
bleat barely audible

like a slow drop into frost

been practicing a few
techniques, not to let it
spot me first, stay
downwind, move when its head

is down feeding (20
seconds maybe to creep
to another spot, count
to 10, wait) know

not to hide (seen it look
at me, think
i'm a tree or a stump) walk
forward, freeze

walk again, freeze, step
by step till the range
is good (seen it

doesn't see the tree
is closer, the bow raised)

& shoot
hard winter, white tail in new
snow

THORLEIFUR JÓAKIMSSON, DAYBOOK VI

january 1, 1877: frosthard
all december, no snowfall
30 minus

today is clear
learned to call

animals to me, mimic
the squeak of a mouse, cry
of a rabbit in pain

with my lips, a long
drawn out kiss
on the back of a wet
hand, squeals

in the brush, a short
smack like a rodent
outside the hole, learned

to pry with a rodent
skewer, willow fork
into the animal's den

through its fur, wind it
tight, learned to flood
mouseholes, 'smack them

with sticks as they flee
out of the ground
frost

penetrates the settlement
ice crystal pitchforks
pry through my skin

(jóhann says worse
lies ahead, the long
drawn out kiss

of a deeper frost
clinging frost, waits

in ambush
somewhere this month)

THORLEIFUR JÓAKIMSSON, DAYBOOK VII

march 1, 1877: snow
3 feet deep all january
dropped in february, sun

up 9½ to 10½ hours now
been preparing bones

of small birds for fish
tackle, for spring
small wishbone hooks

skewer hooks with bone
slivers tied on (the fish
swallows, the bone

twists sideways, holds)
cross hooks, plain hooks
with a thin bone wall
(bird or rodent, cut

in squares, punched in
rings, cut in two
places)

been sharpening, smearing
hook shanks with pitch
ready for spring nettles

for a line, out of the long

nights
when ice loosens, rivers
begin to run

anytime now

THORLEIFUR JÓAKIMSSON, DAYBOOK VIII

april 20, 1877: think
it's spring, snow
gone by yesterday, ice

loosened on icelandic
river, today
18 plus (told jóhann

you can live long
on one small stream
(crayfish, mussels, stone
flies, snails, minnows) have to

get it down, how
to trap the stream
told him mussels are buried

in mud (a shallow trail
a small hump
at the end) told him

take crayfish at night
by hand, frighten them
up (rustle rocks they lie

under)) may 1 he's going

with me, got
a basket trap made, he'll
drown it, i'll

kick stones in the riverbed
every one, he'll lift
the basket full

of edible life, spring
think it's spring

the hump at the end

THORLEIFUR JÓAKIMSSON, DAYBOOK IX

july 1, 1877: the first
rain may 5, grass
sprouts, leaves burst

the first thundershower may
16, the day
wheat was put in, ice

disappeared from the lake
rest of may, continuous
sun, june strong

heat, i'm down
to jerky now, have to
do something with the meat

have to cut it
into strips, dry it
in sun two days, store it

hard & brittle, have to
dry the rabbit whole (skin
eviscerate it

crack the back between
legs, insert a stick
lay it flat

on a rock in sun) pound
crush the bones, dry
the marrow, one more
day, by now

when i walk across the ill
field, my limbs
crack

marrow in my legs
trickles out like sand

counting the days
till fall

THORLEIFUR JÓAKIMSSON, DAYBOOK X

august 27, 1877: heat
dry (small rain
three times only)

discovered pemmican, dried
berries pounded
into paste, mixed

with jerky, melted
suet, meat, stuffed
in a deer's intestine, tied

shut, sealed
with suet, stored in skin
bags soaked

in melted suet (like blood
pudding, liverpaste)

it's the pounding that does it

pounding of berries
jerky, blue, purple

it's my heart on the stone
i pound & pound

but the beating continues

louder each time, stone
on stone, strong
heat, sweat
in my palms

THORGRÍMUR JÓNSSON I

water boatmen

leave gimli september 5
1876 for icelandic
river, 27 of us

on the flat body
of one boat, too
thin, too weak, i row

with my legs in a pool

the summer is in low
tide, my oar too
erratic clings

to submerged trees
roots, weeds (won't last
through a change

of weather) wind

turns, put up sails
(won't make it, already
a few seasick)

have to land, have
to keep it afloat, let
them unload the flour-
sacks, waves

burst out of the current
over my head, water
out of the east crashes
straight into the bank

(won't make it, eight
men & one, jón
from brenniborg, skaga-

fjördur has a lame hand
can't row, has to use
his legs) our boat

fills with water (can't see

land in the east)
the lake's lame lips
broken teeth in the tide:

land it, go ahead, let
the seam rip, the rusty

nails fall out like green
bugs in a pond
land

on their backs, legs
claw the air: just

land, land

THORGRÍMUR JÓNSSON II

lean at
an angle on the bank
head down, drink hot
coffee by a hardwood

fire, cold
wet, need to pitch
camp, construct
a reflector, blue clouds

ripple in the sky, wind
scoops up my fatigue
rain stings

like flies, september
6, rain down
my back, east wind
in

between slow-catching
logs: go look
for the nearest settle-
ment (the rest

wait, heads around
the fire, slow-drying
arms, backswimmers
on the storm) look

for benedikt ólafsson
help for elbowed
knees, slanted

children (september 11

finally we move, north
again to icelandic
river) backswimmers

we move against currents
air & water, forwards

forwards on our backs

THORGRÍMUR JÓNSSON III

measure the land
september 12, long
slender legs walk

¼ mile for each section
four to a mile (4
invisible breathing tubes)

stefán eyjólfsson from
unaós uses a walking
stick, corrects
deviations, curves

september 13, go east
to sandy bar (find
a steamship with a government
loan on board)

the sun lays eggs
on my back, haying

begins september 16
carry bales of hay on
my back (lumps

swell in giant
bites of land)

it's a water scorpion
in sandy bar, with long
hind legs, thin
lungs behind

it won't retract

under the land, my legs
pace east, dry as
grass

THORGRÍMUR JÓNSSON IV

september 24, 1876: smallpox
creeps with brown
toads' legs

out of the clothes jón
from brenniborg bought
in quebec (the same way

black plague arrived
in iceland, 1402) velvet
blue it arrives

on front legs, middle
legs, since

we left home june 30
1876, 30 dead (kids
dead of food at sea)

september 30: 19 dead
of smallpox, black
striding now

winged over water
waterstriders

ripplebugs feed on my
skin, december 11:
thorgerdur, wife of jón

from brenniborg, dead

dead, swarming now
broad-shouldered on
their own, under my clothes

rivers creep, toad
bugs, toads down
my spine

THORGRÍMUR JÓNSSON V

burn out the old year
at grund, jóhann briem's
place, new year's eve
1876, those able

to walk are out

what's left of my
eyes protrudes (can't
fish this winter
smallpox overlaps

into hunting, building)
i'm the hunted now

live under dead
leaves, my people
without time left
to construct (keep going

on government loans)
maybe next year, spring
leaves will stir, fish
burst out

of dead ice, dead
flakes on the ground
maybe what's left

of my people will walk
away from this place

maybe next year

THORGRÍMUR JÓNSSON VI

the printing house
of lundar, east of the river
begins: january 26

1877 (a small milkweed
seed) been to a meeting
in mödruvellir on

a settlement government
(small leaf-footed
bug) been to a meeting

on a district government
in sandy bar february
14 (big-eyed bug)

spring enters my house
broad-headed, the new
government emerges

from the doorway, up

from under decaying
bark, woody fungi
eyes on spines all
over its body (70½

shares already
in the press) jóhann
briem is the district
governor (our first

velvet-water measurer)

we begin
to scrape away

the wingless, eye-
bulging spiny shore
bugs, out

out of my house

begin to press them
down, on paper

THORGRÍMUR JÓNSSON VII

go south to gimli
about the government-
loan cows, july 1

soft-bodied cows
two-colored cows

my wings are grown
back, hind legs
for jumping when i'm
disturbed, still slender

as gnats, head still
constricted behind
my eye-balls, but i'll

recover, beyond wings

(the cows aren't there
yet) return july

23 (at last, august
4, 1877: cows, handed
over on the east bank)

one cow for each
farmer, one cow
nonwinged, nonjumping

ambush cows
from the government (lying
in wait for numbers
to decrease) at last

but this is one
year too late

one year too late

THORGRÍMUR JÓNSSON VIII

july, 1877, icelandic
river: reverend jón
bjarnason from minneapolis
holds service

next day, sandy bar:
been to a meeting to
bring síra jón to sandy
bar (jumping bug

assassin bug, don't like
the shape, the groove
between his eyes)

august 29: heard the decision
to bring jón here
(don't like the segments

on his body, extended
edges of his abdomen
don't want his knife, his

blood-sucking tools, his
walking sticks) síra jón
belongs in the cellar

of an old building (don't
like the segments
divided in sub-segments
one

at the thigh, more
running down his legs
into the ground) jón

belongs in a cellar
with wine, with tools
(don't like his knife

his walking
stick in my eye)

THORGRÍMUR JÓNSSON IX

fishflies live on
the stream, under stones

with front wings, small
clear-winged, clear-
eyed fishbait

(when fish don't bite
they escape)

when you're one you
don't divide

fishflies carry their own
roof with them
wings held over

the body at rest

a beginning: the first
thundershower, the first
wheat under the ground

the first milkweed
cow: a beginning

fish in the stream (i, too

am attracted
to the light, at night

go big-eyed, alone
from under the stone)

i can leave now

Kristjana Gunnars was born in Reykjavik, Iceland, in 1948. She immigrated to Canada in 1969, after doing undergraduate work in Oregon. She has lived in rural British Columbia, Vancouver, Toronto, Winnipeg, and Regina, where she took an M.A. in literature. Gunnars worked as a schoolteacher in rural Iceland in 1973-74, and taught English at the University of Regina from 1976-78. She is now researching the history and literature of Icelandic settlers in Canada. Her poems have appeared in various journals in Canada and the U.S.

Turnstone Press
Settlement Poems 2
by Kristjana Gunnars

This book was designed by Gudrun
Rohatgi. The map reproduced on the cover
is by Professor Gissur Eliasson. The
photograph of Halldór Briem is from *The
Icelandic Canadian*, Summer, 1975.

Turnstone Press
St. John's College
University of Manitoba
Winnipeg, Manitoba
R3T 2M5

Previous Publications from Turnstone Press

In the Gutting Shed by W.D. Valgardson
Open Country by George Amabile
the lands I am by Patrick Friesen
Changehouse by Michael Tregebov
Seems Valuable by Ed Upward
Seed Catalogue by Robert Kroetsch
The Inside Animal by Arthur Adamson
Blowing Dust off the Lens by Jim Wallace
bluebottle by Patrick Friesen
Soviet Poems by Ralph Gustafson
Rehearsal for Dancers by Craig Powell
Mister Never by Miriam Waddington
The Cranberry Tree by Enid Delgatty Rutland
Rock Painter by R.E. Rashley
First Ghost to Canada by Kenneth McRobbie
No Longer Two People by Patrick Lane and Lorna Uher
The Earth Is One Body by David Waltner-Toews
The Man with the Styrofoam Head by Gregory Grace
When the Dogs Bark at Night by Valerie Reed
The Bridge, That Summer by A.E. Ammeter
This Body That I Live In by Anne Le Dressay
Mother's Gone Fishing by Norma Dillon
Almost a Ritual by Les Siemieniuk
Jimmy Bang Poems by Victor Enns
Across the White Lawn by Robert Foster
Shore Lines by Douglas Barbour
No Country for White Men by Gordon Turner
Interstices of Night by Terrence Heath
A Planet Mostly Sea by Tom Wayman
Scarecrow by Douglas Smith
Leaving by Dennis Cooley
The Light of Our Bones by Douglas Smith
Settlement Poems 1 by Kristjana Gunnars
I Want to Tell You Lies by John Lane
Marsh Burning by David Arnason
Humans and Other Beasts by Lorna Uher
Lacuna by Laura McLauchlan
The Shunning by Patrick Friesen
A Game of Angels by Anne Szumigalski
Look the Lovely Animal Speaks by Robert Hilles
A Shored Up House by Elizabeth Allen
While You Were Out by Kate Bitney
Dry Media by Brenda Riches